Community Helpers
Then and Now

Bobbie Kalman

🌳 Crabtree Publishing Company

www.crabtreebooks.com

Created by Bobbie Kalman

For my cousin Marcell Halasz,
who plans to serve his Queen and country
as a soldier

Author and Editor-in-Chief
Bobbie Kalman

Editors
Kathy Middleton
Crystal Sikkens

Photo research
Bobbie Kalman

Design
Bobbie Kalman
Samantha Crabtree
Katherine Berti
Samara Parent (front cover)

Prepress technician
Katherine Berti

Print coordinator
Margaret Amy Salter

Illustrations and reproductions
Barbara Bedell: pages 1, 5 (top), 6 (top), 7 (all except
    top left and bottom left and right), 13, 21
Circa Art: page 5 (bottom right)
Licensed by The Greenwich Workshop, Inc.
    www.greenwichworkshop.com; detail from
    The Country doctor, ©Morgan Weistling: cover,
    page 17; detail from The Family Trade, ©Morgan
    Weistling: page 6 (bottom); detail from End of
    Harvest, ©Morgan Weistling: page 15
Bonna Rouse: page 7 (top left and bottom left and right),
    11, 19 (bottom)

Photographs
Library of Congress: LC-DIG-hec-00085: page 21
    (bottom right)
Thinkstock: pages 9 (left), 19 (top), 22 (top)
Other images by Shutterstock, including cover photographs

Library and Archives Canada Cataloguing in Publication

Kalman, Bobbie, author
        Community helpers then and now / Bobbie Kalman.

(From olden days to modern ways in your community)
Includes index.
Issued in print and electronic formats.
ISBN 978-0-7787-0115-6 (bound).--ISBN 978-0-7787-0143-9 (pbk.).
--ISBN 978-1-4271-9414-5 (pdf).--ISBN 978-1-4271-9408-4 (html)

        1. Occupations--Juvenile literature. 2. Communities--Juvenile
literature. I. Title.

HT675.K352 2013   j331.7'93   C2013-906088-X
                                            C2013-906089-8

Library of Congress Cataloging-in-Publication Data

Kalman, Bobbie.
 Community helpers then and now / Bobbie Kalman.
        pages cm. -- (From olden days to modern ways in your community)
 Includes index.
 ISBN 978-0-7787-0115-6 (reinforced library binding) -- ISBN 978-0-7787-0143-9 (pbk.)
 -- ISBN 978-1-4271-9414-5 (electronic pdf) -- ISBN 978-1-4271-9408-4 (electronic html)
 1. Community life--Juvenile literature. 2. Communities--Juvenile literature. 3.
 Municipal services--Juvenile literature. 4. Human services--Juvenile literature. 5.
 Occupations--Juvenile literature. I. Title.

 HM761.K346 2013
 307--dc23
                                            2013034931

Crabtree Publishing Company

Printed in Canada/012014/BF20131120

www.crabtreebooks.com   1-800-387-7650

Published in Canada
Crabtree Publishing
616 Welland Ave.
St. Catharines, Ontario
L2M 5V6

Published in the United States
Crabtree Publishing
PMB 59051
350 Fifth Avenue, 59th Floor
New York, New York 10118

Published in the United Kingdom
Crabtree Publishing
Maritime House
Basin Road North, Hove
BN41 1WR

Published in Australia
Crabtree Publishing
3 Charles Street
Coburg North
VIC 3058

What is in this book?

Community helpers

What is this community helper called?

A **community** is a place where many people live and work together and share buildings, **services**, and laws. **Community helpers** are people who make communities cleaner, safer, and better. Name some community helpers that you see below.

Community helpers long ago

In the past, there were not as many kinds of community helpers as there are today. Some helpers, such as store owners, supplied people with important things they needed. Some drove wagons. Community helpers called **tradesworkers** were very important because they made things that people needed.

Stagecoach drivers took people from town to town and also delivered the mail.

This **metalworker** made pots, pans, cups, and candleholders.

This woman owned a clothing store in a city. She made the clothes she sold.

Tradesworkers long ago

Before there were machines, tradesworkers made everything by hand using simple tools. **Carpenters**, **wheelwrights**, **harness makers**, and **blacksmiths** were some tradesworkers in old communities.

horseshoe

*Blacksmiths made horseshoes from **iron** to protect the hoofs of horses and oxen. Blacksmiths also made the metal parts of carriage wheels.*

Wagons were repaired in this shop.

harness   saddle

Harness makers used leather to make saddles and harnesses for horses.

Wheelwrights made wagon wheels from wood and iron.

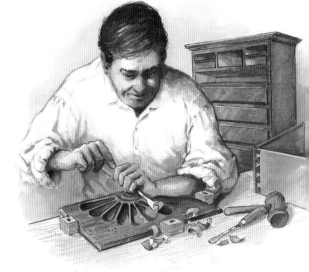

Tradesworkers used simple tools like these.

Coopers made barrels, buckets, and other containers from wood.

Carpenters made furniture from wood. They also helped build homes.

Tradesworkers today

Tradesworkers today are still important community helpers, but what they make and how they do it may be very different from how tradesworkers did it long ago. In the past, for example, wagon-repair workers fixed wagons, and today, **mechanics** fix cars. Tradesworkers today still use some simple tools, but they also use new kinds of machines to do their work.

This mechanic is changing a flat tire.

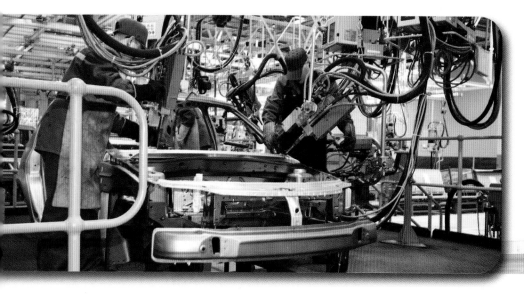

*In the past, parts of wagons were made by hand. Today, cars are made in **factories**. Machines are used to make the parts and put them together.*

This carpenter is using an electric saw to cut wood.

There were no **electricians** in the past because electricity had not yet been invented. This electrician is fixing some wires on a hydro pole.

This tradesperson is a **welder**. Welders join materials, such as metals or plastics, together. This welder uses her laptop to record information about her work.

Do you know?

Which tradesworkers have worked at your home? Why are they important community helpers?

Construction workers

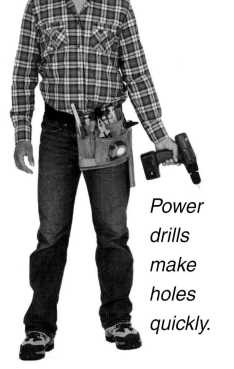

Power drills make holes quickly.

Construction workers are tradesworkers who build homes, offices, schools, hospitals, and many other buildings. They also build roads and bridges. They use many kinds of tools and machines like power drills, cranes, bulldozers, and cement trucks.

Cranes lift objects to high places.

*Cement trucks make **concrete** to use in building homes and roads.*

Bulldozers move dirt.

crane

Builders in the past

Long ago, there were very few machines, so builders used simple tools, such as hammers, saws, and axes. It took a long time to construct a building. After machines were invented, tall buildings could be built quickly.

Long ago, homes were built using hand tools like these.

*In big cities about 100 years ago, builders constructed **skyscrapers** using steel, concrete, and glass. The construction workers of the past did not wear **personal protective equipment**. What safety gear do construction workers wear today?*

11

School helpers

Most of the people who work at your school are teachers, but some school workers help you in other ways. The **principal** is the head of the school. The **librarian** shows you how to find the books you need.

*How many teachers work at your school? How does a school **nurse** help you? Who helps students cross the street? Who drives them to school in a bus?*

Who were the helpers?

Long ago, many schools had only one room and one teacher. Not only did teachers plan lessons and teach their students, they also had to keep the school clean. Students helped them sweep the floor, wash the blackboard, and bring in water from the well. The parents of the students paid the teacher's **salary**.

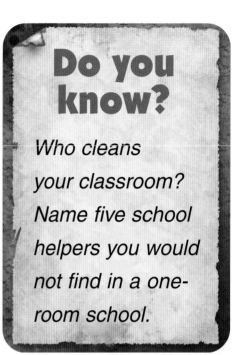

Do you know?

Who cleans your classroom? Name five school helpers you would not find in a one-room school.

Food and farm workers

Farmers grow the foods we eat, such as corn.

Next to air and water, food is the most important thing we need to stay alive. **Agricultural workers**, or farmers, grow the food we eat. The farms send some of the food to factories, where it can be made into different kinds of foods. The foods are then sold in **supermarkets**. Many people help get food from farms to our tables. Who are these helpers?

Workers in factories prepare and package foods, such as bread.

Supermarket workers keep the foods fresh for us to take home.

Drivers deliver the food to stores, where we buy it.

Farming long ago

In the past, most people got their food from gardens they planted next to their homes. People also raised chickens, pigs, and one or two horses and cows. Some farmers had large fields where they grew corn or wheat. Farm helpers were often family members, like the children above collecting pumpkins.

Are you a helper?

Do you have a garden at your home? How do you help care for it? Do you help your parents with grocery shopping or cooking? What can you cook?

Medical helpers

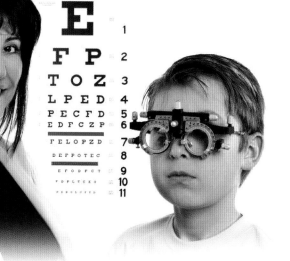

*An **optometrist** checks your eyes and tells you if you need glasses. He or she then makes the glasses you need.*

Medical helpers are nurses, dentists, and many kinds of doctors, who treat different body parts, such as eyes or teeth. The **pharmacist** at your drugstore is another important helper because he or she gives you the medicine you need to get well.

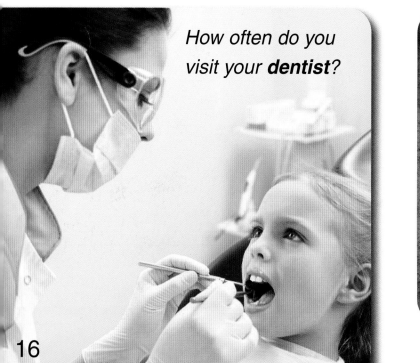

*How often do you visit your **dentist**?*

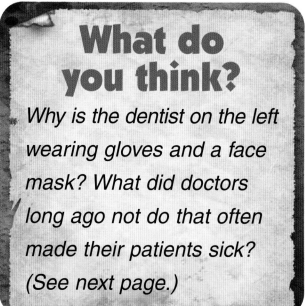

What do you think?

Why is the dentist on the left wearing gloves and a face mask? What did doctors long ago not do that often made their patients sick? (See next page.)

Medical helpers long ago

In the old days, the same doctor that treated your illnesses also looked after your teeth and your eyes. He often traveled from one small community to another to help sick people. In those days, people did not know that **germs** caused many **diseases**. In fact, people thought that taking too many baths could make them sick! Doctors often passed along diseases because they did not wash their hands or the **instruments**, or tools, they used.

Long ago, doctors did not have offices. They came to see sick patients at their homes. This doctor is visiting a sick child. Why might the child be afraid?

First responders

First responders are emergency workers who are the first to **respond**, or act, in **emergencies**. An emergency is a dangerous situation that happens suddenly. First responders include **police officers**, **ambulance** drivers, **paramedics**, and **firefighters**. In emergencies, **911 operators** receive calls from people who need help. They then send emergency workers to where they are needed.

Helicopters fly people quickly to hospitals. Paramedics are trained to keep people alive until they arrive at a hospital where they can receive help from doctors.

No emergency help

In olden times, there were no telephones or emergency numbers to call. There were no first responders, either. When there was an emergency, people helped one another. In big cities, there were hospitals, but their ambulances were pulled by horses.

People could not get to a hospital quickly in a horse-drawn ambulance. Without paramedics, they could not get the help they needed right away.

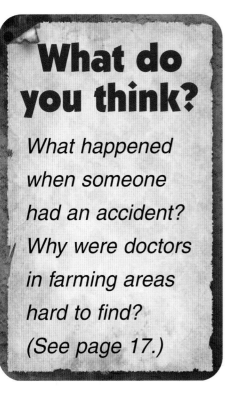

What do you think?

What happened when someone had an accident? Why were doctors in farming areas hard to find? (See page 17.)

Firefighters

Fires can start quickly! Firefighters help fight fires and rescue people and animals. They put out fires that start in buildings. They also fight forest and bush fires. Firefighters today drive big trucks and use water from **fire hydrants** to put out fires. Fire hydrants can be found in many places around towns and cities.

fire hydrant

This firefighter is climbing up a ladder to rescue a person who is trapped inside a burning building.

At a forest or bush fire, firefighters use helicopters to drop buckets of water on burning trees and bushes.

Many fires

Long ago, people used candles for light and fireplaces for cooking and heating homes. Open flames made accidental fires very common. In those days, there were no fire trucks or firefighters, so buckets of water were passed along lines of people to put out the flames of a fire. After cars were invented, firefighters drove fire trucks with pumps, which sprayed water on fires.

People used buckets of water to put out fires. How are buckets still used by firefighters today?

These firefighters are putting out a fire with a hose filled with water that they carried in their trucks. There were no fire hydrants in those days.

Police officers

Police officers protect people in towns and cities. They **patrol**, or drive regularly through, neighborhoods, as well as along highways, to watch for people who are breaking the law. They also help people who need help.

Long ago, some criminals were locked up in jail wagons like this.

This police officer has been called to someone's home. Name some reasons why people need help from the police.

Learn more

Books

Crabtree, Marc. (Meet my neighbor series). Crabtree Publishing, 2009–2013.

Flatt, Lizann. *Life in a Farming Community* (Learn about Rural Life). Crabtree Publishing, 2010.

Kalman, Bobbie. *My Community Long Ago* (My World). Crabtree Publishing, 2011.

Kalman, Bobbie. *Helpers in my community* (My World) Crabtree Publishing, 2010.

Kalman, Bobbie. *A Visual Dictionary of a Pioneer Community* (Crabtree Visual Dictionaries). Crabtree Publishing, 2008.

Kalman, Bobbie. (My Community and its Helpers series). Crabtree Publishing, 2005.

Kalman, Bobbie and Niki Walker. *Community Helpers from A to Z* (AlphaBasiCs). Crabtree Publishing, 1998.

Kalman, Bobbie. *A One-Room School* (Historic Communities). Crabtree Publishing, 1994.

Websites

Ask an adult to help you make these community helper crafts:
www.dltk-kids.com/crafts/miscellaneous/ communities.htm

Watch this video to learn more about community helpers:
www.youtube.com/watch?v=5fSrq4k6UXk

Learn more about one-room schools long ago at:
www.aitc.sk.ca/saskschools/school.html

Words to know

Note: Some boldfaced words are defined where they appear in the book.

concrete A mixture of cement, sand or pebbles, and water, used in buildings or other structures

disease A condition in a person's body that makes him or her sick

factory A building where things are made by machines and people

fire hydrant A covered pipe above ground that is connected to water underground. Hoses can be attached to fire hydrants to fight fires.

germs Tiny organisms that can cause diseases

iron A grayish-white metal used for making horseshoes and other things

nurse A person trained to care for sick or injured people

personal protective equipment Safety gear that is worn to help protect a person from injury

salary Money paid to a person regularly for doing a job

service A job or helpful act

stagecoach A large, closed carriage pulled by horses, used long ago for carrying people, mail, or goods

supermarket A large store that sells food; also called a grocery store

Index